ACKNOWLEDGEMENTS

Any craft book is the result of a concerted joint effort, and
Details, Details is no exception. I am indebted to the creative and
editorial teams at New Holland who have put it all together, especially
Rosemary Wilkinson who invited me to undertake the project in the first
place. Clare Hubbard has steadfastly guided me through to the end, whilst
Amy Corbett has proved an equally good hand model and editorial
assistant. Thanks too to Samantha Gray. Sian Irvine's wonderful
photographs, along with Isobel Gillan's design skills have made this
into a really special book. Finally, I must thank my family – as ever –
and also my long-standing friend Lis Gunner for giving so freely
of her time and ideas.

detailsdetails

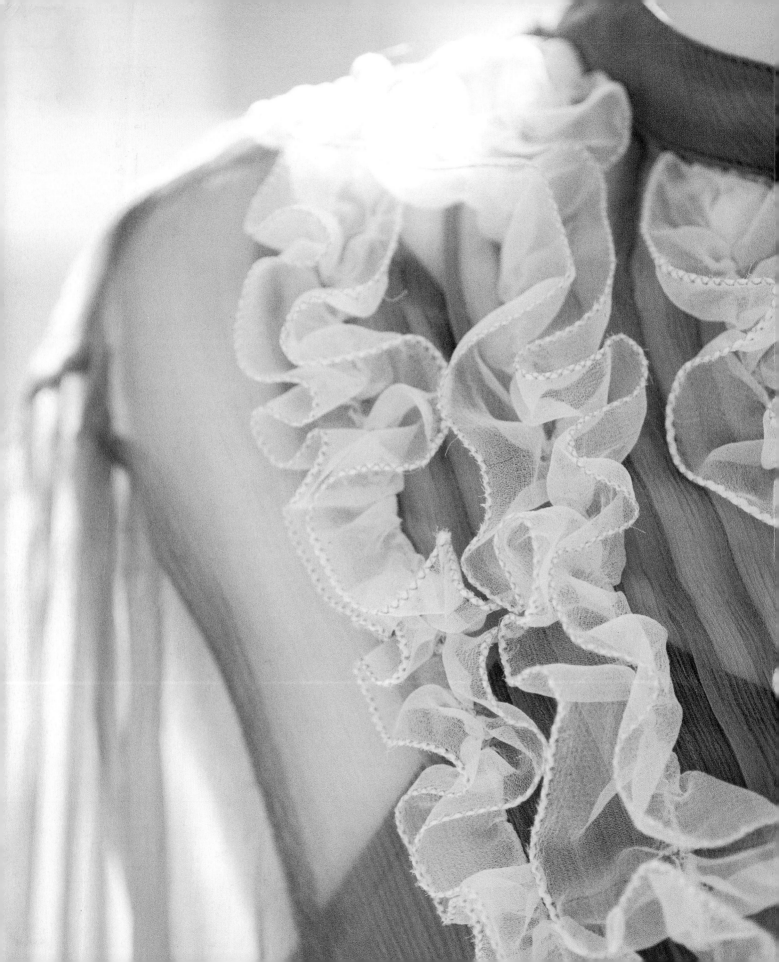

detailsdetails

EMBELLISHING CLOTHES AND ACCESSORIES

LUCINDA GANDERTON

NEW HOLLAND

Published in 2007 by
New Holland Publishers (UK) Ltd
London · Cape Town · Sydney · Auckland

Garfield House,
86-88 Edgware Road
London, W2 2EA
United Kingdom
www.newhollandpublishers.com

80 McKenzie Street, Cape Town 8001
South Africa

Unit 1, 66 Gibbes Street, Chatswood, NSW 2067
Australia

218 Lake Road, Northcote, Auckland
New Zealand

ISBN 978 1 84537 730 4

Senior Editor: Clare Hubbard
Editorial Direction: Rosemary Wilkinson
Photography: Sian Irvine
Design: Isobel Gillan
Illustrations: Stephen Dew
Production: Hazel Kirkman

10 9 8 7 6 5 4 3 2 1

Reproduction by Colour Scan, Singapore
Printed and bound by Craft Print International,
  Singapore

A special mention should go to Berwick Offray and
DMC who generously supplied many of the ribbons
and the embroidery threads used in the projects.

Note: The author and publishers have made every
effort to ensure that all instructions given in this
book are safe and accurate, but they cannot accept
liability for any resulting injury or loss or damage to
either property or person, whether direct or
consequential and howsoever arising.

contents

introduction

In the ever-changing world of style, there is one constant rule: in time all trends fall out of favour, but they invariably reappear – sometimes many years later – as the latest, most desirable fashion.

street chic

After decades of minimalism, decorative detailing is once again popular. Interiors magazines are full of patterned wallpaper and furnishing fabrics while, in the world's couture capitals, designers are sending models down the catwalk in garments adorned with every trimming imaginable, from ribbons, feathers and lace to beads and crystals. These key trends are reflected in high street stores, which are brimming with embellished clothing and accessories.

crafty techniques

Today's fashion is eclectic, a vibrant mix of colours and themes which draw inspiration from world cultures, historical costume and modern innovation. New laser-cut edgings mimic delicate lace, and printing techniques can reproduce intricate stitching. There has also been a revival of traditional needlework techniques, including hand embroidery, crochet and patchwork, which are once again appreciated for their unique qualities. Many fashion collections feature appliquéd lace motifs, beadwork and shimmering sequins. The look can be easily reproduced at home if you want to jazz up your existing clothes, revamp a vintage find or transform a plain top into something special.

all the trimmings

Fashion insiders know that adding eyecatching detail is an effective way to emphasise the cut of a tailored garment, enhance a patterned fabric or draw attention to a pretty neckline. It is also a means of expressing your own personality and individual style. Depending on your taste, you may choose a subtle addition, for example, a narrow braid edging on a satin camisole or something a little more flamboyant such as a cascade of ruffles down a silk blouse. On a more practical note, a few beads or a length of ribbon can even be used to conceal an indelible mark, a moth hole or an extended hemline.

finishing touches

Wearing garments you have embellished yourself makes you look completely original – something that cannot otherwise be achieved even by spending a fortune on designer labels. The same is true of accessories. A customized bag, belt or hat boosts a tired dress and transforms an outfit instantly. It is a fashion truism that you can never have too many accessories, so look out for scarves, bags and baskets, hair decorations and gloves in thrift shops and bargain stores, then think of ways in which they can be given a makeover.

do-it-yourself

Whatever your style, I hope that you will find plenty of ideas in this book that will inspire you. The projects are designed to appeal to everybody from the novice to the experienced crafts enthusiast, and you will find that many of them are not as complicated as they may appear at first glance. They range from quick, no-sew solutions such as simply ironing on photographic images to intricate beading. To guide you through each project there are step-by-step instructions and photographs, and in the Practicalities section (see pages 102–105), you can find out how to work the embroidery and sewing stitches involved.

materials and equipment

sourcing your materials

Once you start hunting for decorative trimmings with which to embellish your clothes, you will discover many unexpected sources. If you are a hoarder you may already have a collection of textiles and oddments, and real magpies know that even the tiniest fragment of lace can be recycled. A local craft shop or the fabric and haberdashery departments of a big store may be your next stop, but unique treasures can also be unearthed at upholstery suppliers, vintage fabric fairs or local charity shops. The Internet is now an international market-place where you will find specialist dealers from around the world, and a few of the best websites are listed on pages 110–111.

fabrics

The projects in the following chapters require only small quantities of fabric. Most stores will sell short lengths of 20cm (8in), but look out too for remnants, patchwork pieces and sample swatches. You should always launder new fabrics and garments before embarking on a project to allow for any shrinkage and, as a rule, match similar fibres and weights. Patterned fabrics – floral prints, checks or stripes – can transform a plain garment, whether you are adding new cuffs, cut-out broderie perse motifs or a row of brightly coloured hearts.

You do not always need to spend money on new fabrics, however, and most dressmakers have their

own treasured ragbag, full of offcuts and scraps. Unworn parts of old garments or outgrown children's clothing can be salvaged and transformed into appliqué shapes, and beautiful fabric from an outdated skirt can be cut up and used again.

beads, sequins and buttons

Beads and sequins come in every colour imaginable, and can be used to create interesting textures and patterns, for lettering, or to outline motifs. Small round glass rocailles and tube-like bugles come in metallic, clear, opaque or frosted finishes and are most commonly used for embroidery. Larger beads, including faceted crystals, faux pearls and tear-shaped drop beads, create highlights, imitate petals or can be used to form geometric shapes within a design. Re-use beads from broken or budget-priced jewellery too – for example, the pearl discs used on the Beaded kaftan top (see pages 16–17) were originally part of a bargain bracelet. Tumbled gemstone chips and seed pearls, available from jewellery suppliers, are an unusual alternative to glass beads. Sequins add glitter and can be used in combination with beads or on their own to form all-over designs. A matching set of new buttons will revamp a jacket instantly, while the assorted contents of a button tin can be ideal for decorating a bag or a pair of trousers, or for incorporating as part of an embroidered design. Always keep the buttons and trimmings from a discarded garment – you never know when they will come in useful.

lace, ribbons and braids

Frothy, delicate lace has a period charm all of its own but, used imaginatively, it can also look contemporary. There are many traditional types, each with a unique look. White cotton broderie anglaise is crisp and smart, while black lace has an undeniable glamour. Versatile guipure lace, like the daisy chain trimming

on pages 72–73, is made up of individually woven motifs that can be snipped apart and used separately. Heavier torchon lace is ideal for edging summer skirts and petticoats (see page 44).

Ribbon has an enormous variety of uses and is available in countless patterns, shades and widths: ribbed petersham is ideal for hat bands and trimming heavier garments, double-face satin makes the best rosettes and bows, and wire-edged ribbon is perfect for making three-dimensional flowers. Tiny ready-made ribbon flowers and bows are excellent for a quick makeover. Loosely woven organza or silk embroidery ribbon, softer than satin ribbon, is fine enough to be stitched to form intricate petals.

Patterned woven braids, including those intended for furnishing, give a luxurious finish to winter clothing and outerwear. Visit specialist Indian fabric shops to find the most exciting versions: hand-beaded trims, metallic sari braids and intricately woven floral or paisley designs. Wavy ricrac has long been a

children's favourite and is once again fashionable. It has been used by generations of mothers to disguise a let-down hem, but it is also perfect for giving a light-hearted touch to your own garments.

threads and yarns

All-purpose polyester or cotton sewing thread comes in reels of 100 metres (110 yards) up to 500 metres (546 yards) for the serious dressmaker. It is designed for hand or machine stitching natural or synthetic fabrics, and is also used for appliqué and beadwork. Always match the colour to your fabric as closely as possible and, when stitching on beads, choose a shade to match the background rather than the beads themselves.

Embroidery threads come in a spectrum of colours and assorted finishes and thicknesses. Stranded cotton is a loosely twisted six-strand thread, sold in hanks bound with paper bands. Use one or two

strands for fine work and all six for chunkier stitches; you can mix different coloured strands for subtle effects. Metallic threads look good with beads and sequins. Soft embroidery cotton, also known as *coton â brodé* is made of five tightly twisted strands that do not separate. It has a matte finish and is ideal for bold designs on cotton knits. Pearl cotton or *coton perlé* comes in three weights and has a mercerised finish, which gives the stitches a shiny appearance.

In addition you can use tapestry yarn for embroidering on woollen fabrics such as tweed or felt. This soft wool comes in an array of colours and can also be used to make braided trimmings (see the Braided tweed jacket on pages 94–96). Finally, there are many knitting yarns to choose from and the range of colour and effects is constantly being expanded. Even if you do not wish to knit with them, they can be plaited or couched to create fluid outlines.

sewing kit

All the equipment you need to get started is the basic tool kit of needles, pins, scissors and a tape measure, which can be stored in anything from a purpose-made workbox, with individual compartments for each item, to an empty biscuit tin. As you become more experienced, you will find other more specialised accessories, such as an embroidery hoop, are useful. There is a wide choice of sewing machines available, many with complicated computer programmes. Only a straightforward model is needed, however, for the straight and zigzag stitches used for the projects in this book.

pins and needles

Steel dressmaker's pins are used to pin two edges together before seaming or to attach motifs or lace to a garment before stitching down. Always remove them after tacking or sewing, and replace in their box or pincushion.

Needles seem to come in a bewildering range of sizes and shapes, but each has its own special purpose. General sewing needles, called sharps, have small round eyes and are used for hand stitching and tacking. Crewel needles have long eyes to accommodate stranded embroidery threads, while thicker chenille needles are used for heavier threads and yarns. Blunt tapestry needles are needed to stitch on knitted fabrics, as they do not split the fibres. The larger the number on the packet, the shorter and finer the needle itself. You will need sizes 10–12 for stitching and threading small beads. Keep your needles to hand in a needle book – they tend to disappear into the filling when plunged into a pincushion.

cutting out

It is helpful to have three pairs of scissors, each with a specific purpose. Small embroidery scissors have narrow pointed blades for clipping threads, cutting out motifs and trimming seams. Medium-sized sewing scissors are easier to manage than large shears and will cut fabrics accurately. Paper will blunt any blades, so keep a pair of household scissors just for making templates.

marking and measuring

A strong, flexible tape measure is essential for measuring fabric, and a clear ruler is useful for checking hems as well as drawing lines. You will need a sharp pencil for tracing cut out templates. To draw round the templates on to fabric you will need a dressmaker's pen, which produces a fading or water-soluble line, or a chalk marking pencil that can be brushed away for use on darker fabrics. A transfer pencil and tracing paper are useful for tracing an intricate motif. The drawn lines are then transferred directly on to fabric by ironing from the wrong side.

special papers

There are three comparatively new products that will help you to achieve a professional-looking result and create imaginative designs. Bonding web is a timesaving innovation for creating appliqué designs. Follow the manufacturer's instructions to add cut out motifs to garments – you can then stitch around the edges by hand or machine to make them more durable. Tear-off backing paper gives support to dense embroidery stitches or machine appliqué and prevents the garment from becoming distorted while you are working. Photo-transfer paper can be used to transfer any printed image on to fabric, offering endless exciting possibilities for adding photographs or drawings to your garments. Photo-transfer paper is available from good stationers and computer suppliers in two types, for use on either dark or light fabrics. Local print shops or photocopiers can print on laser transfer paper for you if you do not have the necessary equipment at home.

11

beads and sequins

Sparkling sequins and glass beads – as well as gleaming pearls – have an opulent quality that inspired the six projects in this chapter. Garments ranging from denim jeans to a delicate silk top and ballerina cardigan can be enhanced with simple beadwork embroidery techniques. Discover, too, how the existing stitching on bargain buys such as a cotton kaftan top or the floral design on a 50s-style skirt can be used as the basis for beautiful beaded designs, and how to transform a cashmere shrug with a golden butterfly.

retro floral skirt

This 1950s-style pleated skirt provides the perfect showcase for a long-hoarded collection of sequins, beads and tiny velvet flowers. They add an element of fun and surprise to the large-scale floral print.

YOU WILL NEED

cotton skirt with printed border
   of flowers
sewing kit
matching sewing thread
rocaille beads in colours to
   match the print
velvet flowers
flower-shaped sequins
small clear green drop beads

1 Thread a fine needle and sew a cluster of rocaille beads to the centre of a flower (see page 105). Here, bronze rocailles are stitched to the centre of a rose. Add a scattering of different-coloured beads – for this design, pale gold ones were used – at the end of the stamens.

3 Add a scattering of rocaille beads to give highlights of colour, then sew small green drop beads around the flowers to give the impression of fine leaves.

2 Arrange the velvet flowers on the design, using a rocaille bead to anchor each one in place. Add a few more beads around the centre of the larger printed flowers, then group flower sequins around them.

beaded kaftan top

A loose cotton top is an essential cover-up for every holiday wardrobe. Look out for a plain kaftan with self-coloured embroidery and transform it into something special by picking out details of the design with intricate beadwork.

YOU WILL NEED

cotton kaftan top with
  embroidered yoke
sewing kit
matching sewing thread
6mm (¼in) oval beads in
  three toning colours
2mm (¹⁄₁₂in) pearlescent
  rocaille beads in two
  colours
4mm (¹⁄₁₆in) brass beads
12mm (½in) pearl discs
8mm (⅓in) metal discs

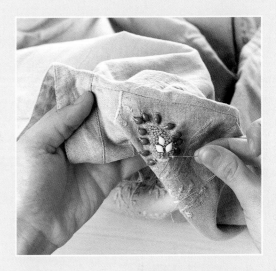

1 Sew oval beads in the centre of each motif, and around the outside edges, following the lines of the embroidery (see page 105).

2 Fill in all the motifs with rocaille beads, stitching them closely together to conceal the background fabric.

3 Embellish the central motif with large and small beads. Sew on a few pearl and metal discs around the yoke to add highlights to the finished design.

shimmering evening top

Well-cut garments, such as this layered silk top, need little extra decoration. Emphasise the delicate fabric and the fashionable, high waistline with just a few carefully placed rows of beads and sequins along the hems and seams.

1 Using a fine needle, and thread in a shade to match the garment, sew a line of single rocaille beads along both edges of the sleeves and around the hem (see page 105). Space the beads evenly, at approximately 6mm (¼in) intervals.

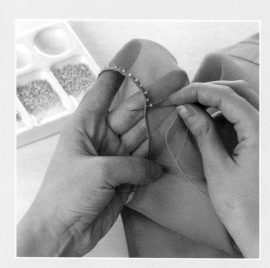

YOU WILL NEED
high-waisted top
sewing kit
matching sewing thread
2mm (¹⁄₁₂in) rocaille beads in two colours
6mm (¼in) translucent cup sequins
4mm (⅛in) opaque cup sequins
8mm (⅓in) translucent cup sequins

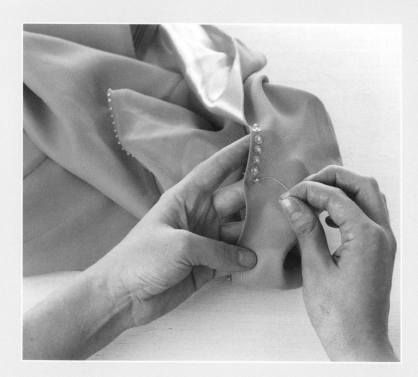

2 Starting at the point of the v-neck, sew a row of evenly spaced 6mm (¼in) translucent sequins up to the seam line, anchoring each one with a rocaille bead in the same colour (see page 105). Repeat on the other side of the neck.

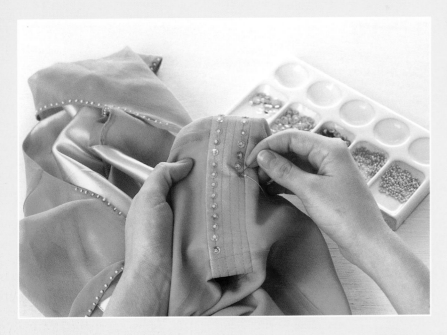

3 Stitch a row of 6mm (¼in) translucent sequins along both edges of the waistband, 6mm (¼in) from the seam. Space the sequins approximately 8mm (⅓in) apart, and anchor each one with a matching rocaille bead.

4 Sew a 4mm (⅙in) opaque sequin at the centre point of the waistband, between the rows of translucent sequins. Add six more of these opaque sequins in a circle around the first to form a small flower.

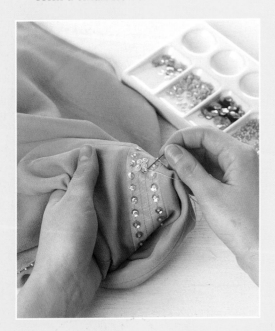

5 Measure 12mm (½in) from the flower and, at this point, anchor an 8mm (⅓in) translucent sequin with a 4mm (⅙in) opaque sequin and a bead. Continue, adding alternate 'flowers' and large sequins as far as the centre back. Decorate the other half of the waistband in the same way.

butterfly shrug

This jewel-like butterfly is deceptively easy to stitch, and the finished effect is stunning.
The pearl beads match the soft jade cashmere exactly, while the glittering gold and green
glass beads add a vibrant sparkle.

1 Trace and cut out the butterfly template on page 106. Place it on the right side of the backing fabric and draw around the edge with a fabric marker pen. Following the manufacturer's instructions, fix the fabric on to the muslin with fusible bonding web. Mount the muslin in a hoop. Outline and fill in the body of the butterfly with dark glass beads, then outline its wings with the light-coloured beads (see page 105).

YOU WILL NEED
fine knit shrug
sewing kit
thin paper and pencil
rectangle of backing fabric,
    approximately 8 × 12cm
    (3 × 4in), to match beads
fabric marker pen
fusible bonding web
muslin to fit embroidery hoop
embroidery hoop
3mm (⅛in) glass beads in a dark
    shade and a light one
four 6mm (¼in) matching pearls
12 matching and 14 contrasting
    4mm (⅛in) pearls
twelve 3mm (⅛in) matching
    pearls

2 Sew a 6mm (¼in) pearl to each marked point on the butterfly's wings. Add a circle of seven 4mm (⅛in) contrasting pearls to the lower wings. Bring up the needle at the centre of one upper wing. Thread on a 4mm (¼in) matching pearl followed by a small one and a dark glass bead, then take the needle down. Repeat five more times to make a six-point star.

3 Fill in the remaining space with the light-coloured glass beads. Remove the completed motif from the frame and cut out carefully, as close to the beaded outline as possible.

4 Pin the butterfly in position on the shoulder of the shrug, then secure with tiny over stitches (see page 103) around the border, close to the beads.

5 As a finishing touch, sew four dark glass beads to either side of the butterfly's head to make its antennae.

23

silver-beaded jeans pockets

Give a designer look to a pair of plain denim jeans by adding bead embroidery to the back pockets. The bugle beads take on a rippling, ribbon-like effect when stitched in rows and the small silver beads look like tiny metal studs.

YOU WILL NEED

pair of jeans with plain
    pockets
sewing kit
tracing paper and pencil
white fabric marker
matching sewing thread
8mm (⅓in) silver twisted
    bugle beads
2mm (¹⁄₁₂in) silver round
    beads

1 Trace the template on page 107 and cut it out carefully. Pin the pattern centrally to one pocket and draw around the outline with a white fabric marker.

2 Thread a fine needle with a long length of thread and knot both ends together. Take the needle through at the centre point of the design and begin stitching on the bugle beads vertically (see page 105). Stagger the beads to follow the outline of the design and continue as far as the first line of stitching. Embellish the remaining three curves in the same way.

3 Following the same curves, finish the design by adding four rows of silver round beads. Space them approximately 3mm (⅛in) from the bugle beads and 3mm (⅛in) apart. Decorate the other pocket in a similar fashion.

ballerina cardigan

A unifying colour scheme in shades of coral, pink, lilac and crimson pulls together the random selection of beads and sequins that decorate the ribbed border of this versatile cardigan.

YOU WILL NEED
wrap-around cardigan
sewing kit
matching sewing thread
selection of toning beads,
    including long and short
    bugles, rocailles, 6mm (¼in)
    crystals and a few diamantés
two 8mm (⅓in) round glass
    beads
petersham ribbon to fit around
    border

1 Stitch a random selection of beads and diamantés around the ribbed border (see page 105). Sew them on singly, as far as the top of the ties on the right side and level with the side opening on the left. Support the finished beadwork by sewing a band of petersham ribbon to the wrong side of the border.

3 Secure the strand with a few stitches into the edge of the tie. Make four more strands in the same way to complete the tassel. Repeat for the other tie.

2 Gather the short end of one tie. Thread on an 8mm (⅓in) glass bead, followed by a rocaille, a short bugle, a rocaille, a long bugle, a rocaille, a short bugle, a faceted crystal and, finally, four rocailles. Take the needle back through the fourth bugle from the end, then through the other beads.

accessories

beaded buttons

To transform or update a cardigan, jacket or coat, easy-to-use kits for fabric-covered buttons are ideal, and come with full instructions. Kits are available in a range of sizes from 12mm (½in) to around 4cm (1¾in) in diameter. The buttons can be covered with fabric to match, or contrast with, the garment (as on the Corsage jacket, pages 61–63). To make these sweet-like beaded versions, stitch on tiny rocailles to cover the background fabric completely.

sequinned belt

An antique cut-steel buckle found in a tin of buttons was the inspiration for this vintage-style belt, which is decorated with old and new sequins. A single strand of metallic embroidery thread was used to stitch the sequins on to a length of dusky plum velvet ribbon. The larger sequins are attached with four to six long stitches radiating from the centre to make a star shape, and the small ones with a single stitch. Before sewing the buckle in place, the velvet ribbon was backed with petersham. For an even quicker and easier alternative, use a ready-made fabric belt.

button bag

A plain canvas tote bag is transformed with a collection of old buttons arranged closely together and stitched in place with thread that matches the background. Such a random approach works best with a limited range of colours – these buttons are predominantly blue and green, with a few complementary yellow and orange highlights. A fabric belt, purse or even a beret could be given the same decorative treatment.

fabric flower brooch

This striking brooch is made in a similar way to the beaded buttons, using an old coat button as the foundation. Cut a circle of embroidered furnishing silk, or other patterned fabric, twice the diameter of the button, with your chosen motif in the centre. For this flower design, tiny beads were used to fill in alternate petals, while a ring of sequins and a larger bead decorate the centre. Gather the edge of the fabric, draw it up tightly over the button and sew on a brooch backing.

ribbon and lace

Many varying effects, ranging from the understated to the extravagant, are possible using ribbons, braids and lace. On the following pages, find out how to lift a garment out of the ordinary with a beaded trim, add multicoloured stripes of ribbon to a denim jacket and apply panels of broderie anglaise to create a romantic blouse. The gores of a long, flared skirt act as a guide for a ribbon and braid design that lends a theatrical flourish, while pretty details such as silk roses and seed pearls are ideal for a delicate camisole. Finally, a project for a summer skirt shows how to create an eyecatching effect with deep lace edging.

classic twin set

Update a pastel twin set of cardigan and short-sleeved jumper by adding co-ordinating beaded trims. You can then use the twin set as versatile separates or wear both garments together for maximum style impact.

1 Starting at the centre back, hand stitch the 12mm (½in) wide trim to the neckband of the jumper using a matching thread. Gather the straight edge slightly so that the trim lies flat around the curves. At the centre back, allow an extra 12mm (½in) and fold under. Stitch the folded edge to the underlying trim carefully so that the join is concealed.

2 Neaten one end of the scalloped trim by turning under the raw edge and stitching it down. Sew the neatened end to the bottom front edge of the cardigan, just inside the ribbed band. Slip stitch (see page 102) the straight edge in place all around the opening. Snip into the scalloped edge so that the braid lies flat at the angle where the button bands meet the V-neck. Work a second line of stitching around the scallops.

bohemian winter skirt

Long strips of woven braid and toning ribbon have been strategically placed on this full-length skirt to emphasise the flared cut and strong vertical lines. The left-overs make the perfect trim for a matching velour hat!

1 Position two lengths of different-coloured ribbon 4mm (⅙in) apart along the diagonal edge of one side panel, following the seam line to the centre panel. Tack in place, then machine stitch on a narrow zigzag setting along both edges of each ribbon using matching thread. Start each line of stitching from the hem to avoid puckering.

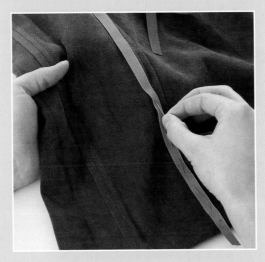

YOU WILL NEED
long panelled skirt
sewing kit
matching sewing thread
sewing machine
8mm (⅓in) wide petersham
   ribbon in two toning colours
6cm (2½in) wide woven braid

2 Pin the braid along the edge of the centre panel, overlapping the ends of the ribbons. Tuck under the raw edge at the waist, tack along each side of the braid and machine stitch. Fold the end over to the wrong side of the hem and hand stitch in place. Decorate the other side of the panel in the same way.

ribbon-yoke denim jacket

No matter what the latest look dictated by style writers may be, denim never really goes out of fashion. To give a favourite denim jacket a new lease of life, hand stitch rainbow stripes of braid and ribbon across the yoke.

YOU WILL NEED
denim jacket
sewing kit
selection of 40cm (16in) lengths
 of 10 ribbons and braids in
 different widths
matching sewing threads

1 Lay the various ribbons across one side of the jacket yoke, changing the positions until you are pleased with the arrangement. Alternate plain colours with patterns, and try placing narrow braids across wide ribbons to vary the effect.

2 Remove the ribbons, keeping them in the correct order. Starting at the lower edge, pin the first length just above the horizontal seam.

3 Tack the ribbon in place, removing the pins as you stitch. Trim the two ends to 6mm (¼in) and tuck them under neatly.

4 Slip stitch the ribbon in place with matching thread (see page 102). Start each line of stitching from the same end to prevent the ribbon becoming puckered. Remove the tacking thread.

5 Sew the remaining ribbons and braids in place, adjusting their lengths to fit the curve at the shoulder seam. Decorate the second part of the yoke in the same way.

broderie anglaise blouse

Lace decoration does not always have to be frilly: used with discretion it can also look smart and elegant. Panels of broderie anglaise, with its characteristic whitework and eyelet embroidery, give a crisply tailored look to this linen blouse.

1 Place the blouse on a flat surface and lay four lengths of broderie anglaise insertion in vertical bands along one front panel. Rearrange the insertions until you are pleased with the design, then make a note of the order in which they lie. Here a narrow lace was positioned by the button band, followed by alternate lengths of wide, then narrow, lace.

YOU WILL NEED

white blouse
sewing kit
3m (3¼yds) × 1.5cm (⅔in) wide
    broderie anglaise insertion
1.5m (1⅔yds) × 2cm (¾in) wide
    broderie anglaise insertion
3m (3¼yds) × 3.5cm (1½in)
    wide broderie anglaise
    insertion
3m (3¼yds) × 12mm (½in) wide
    broderie anglaise edging
white sewing thread
sewing machine
iron

2 Tack the first narrow insertion to the front panel, 8mm (⅓in) from the inside edge of the button band. Fold under a 12mm (½in) turning at each end. Machine stitch along both edges of the insertion, using a narrow zigzag stitch and white thread. Follow the edges closely and start each line of stitching from the hem to prevent puckering.

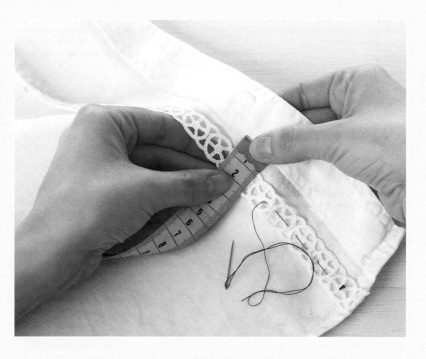

3 Add the remaining three insertions in the same way. Tack the wide insertions in place along both sides before machine stitching in place. Stitch the narrow edging to each edge of the buttonhole band.

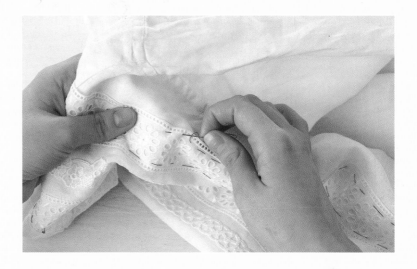

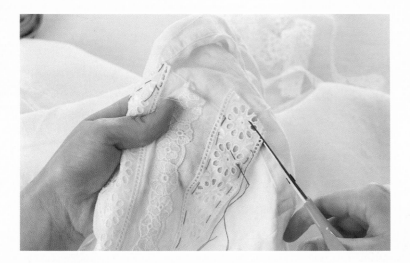

4 Neaten the lace at the shoulder seam by trimming the overlap to 6mm (¼in), turning it under carefully and tacking in place. Slip stitch along the fold and around the ends of the lace (see page 102). Decorate the other front panel in the same way.

5 At the hem of the blouse, secure the surplus lace to the wrong side with small, neat hand stitches. Remove all the tacking threads and press lightly.

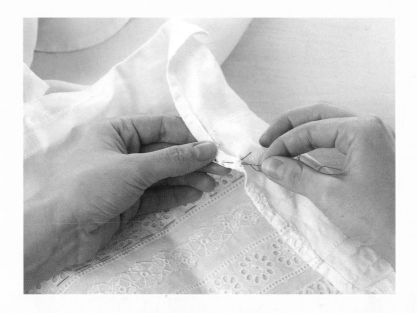

rose and seed pearl camisole

Inspired by the glamorous undergarments of past generations, this feminine camisole is adorned with delicate ribbon roses, silk braid and – as a luxurious finishing touch – the tiniest of seed pearls in palest cream.

YOU WILL NEED
cream silk camisole
sewing kit
1m (39in) narrow ribbon braid
matching sewing thread
8 ribbon roses or other flower
    motifs
beading needle
about seventy 3mm (⅛in) pearl
    beads

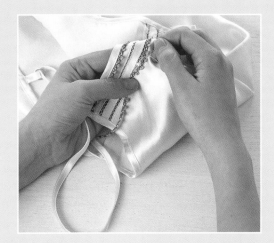

1 Hand sew two lengths of ribbon braid around the neckline, one just below the top edge and the other about 2.5cm (1in) further down. Work with matching sewing thread and keep the stitches as small as possible.

3 Use a fine beading needle to stitch a scattering of pearls around the ribbon roses (see page 105).

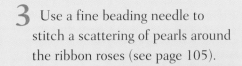

2 Sew a ribbon rose to the base of each shoulder strap, then arrange the other six across the yoke. Mark their positions with pins, then secure each one in place with a few small stitches.

lacy summer skirt

Three different types of lace have been added to this gathered toile skirt: a heavy torchon turns the cotton lining into a pretty petticoat; rounds of fine insertion enliven the yoke and a narrow edging circles the full hem.

1 Pin and tack a line of insertion lace around the bottom edge of the yoke. Machine stitch in place, sewing as close to the edge of the lace as possible. Add another three rounds in the same way, spacing them evenly. Finish the raw ends neatly by turning them under at the zip. Remove the tacking threads at the end of each step.

YOU WILL NEED
gathered skirt with fitted yoke
  and underskirt
sewing kit
2.5cm (1in) wide insertion lace
matching sewing thread
sewing machine
12mm (½in) wide edging lace
8cm (3in) wide torchon lace

2 Position the narrow edging around the skirt hem so that just the embroidered part peeps out from beneath the fold. Pin and tack in place, trimming the ends and turning them under before machine stitching.

3 Cut a length of wide torchon lace to fit around the hem of the underskirt. Pin and tack in place, neatening the ends as necessary, then machine stitch.

accessories

lacy gloves

Guipure lace, which is made up of self-contained motifs (see the Daisy cardigan on pages 72–73) is ideal for lace appliqué as there are no raw edges to fray. These elegant gloves are decorated with two single shapes cut from a deep border lace, one of which is reversed to make a matching pair. Pin, then tack the lace motifs in position and secure them around the outside edges by over stitching in a matching thread (see page 103). Carefully unpick the tacking threads.

vintage clutch bag

Unashamedly nostalgic, this plain organza clutch bag has been given a vintage look using a collection of lace, ribbons and braids left over from previous projects. Arrange the lengths symmetrically then slip stitch them in place (see page 102), starting at the centre and working outwards towards each edge. Tuck under the raw ends neatly and disguise the zip with a frill of lace around the top edge. To finish, add a small bow and a velvet flower stitched in place with a pearl.

beautiful bangles

Cheap wooden or plastic bangles are readily available and fun to transform. Don't worry about the colour - look out for the size and shape you want, then bind the bangle with ribbon or braid. To make sure this stays securely in place, line the inside of the bangle with a narrow strip of double-sided tape. Wrap the ribbon or braid at an angle, pulling it tightly so that the edges lie side by side. A hair band could be given the same treatment.

ribbon rosettes

No longer reserved for gymkhanas or canvassing politicians, rosettes can now be seen on the smartest lapels and hair ties! This one is made from a chequered ribbon that is darker along one edge. Cut a 30cm (12in) length, secure the ends together and run a gathering stitch along one edge, pulling up the gathers to form a circle. Then cut a 25m (10in) length and run a gathering stitch along the opposite - light or dark - edge, pulling up the gathers tightly to make a slightly smaller circle. Place this over the first circle and sew the two together through the centre, adding a button or bead to hide the stitching. To make the tails, cut three 15cm (6in) lengths of matching satin ribbon, trim the ends diagonally, and stitch to the centre back of the rosette.

patches and scraps

With imagination, scraps of almost any fabric may be used to create the extra details that add colour, texture or pattern to garments. Silk organza ruffles, torn strips of cotton lawn, brightly coloured heart motifs, textured fabric strips, offcuts of Welsh tweed turned into a corsage and Provençale prints made into rosettes are all used on the following pages to transform a variety of basic garments. Haberdashery items, such as buttons and ricrac braid, occasionally complement a theme and add highlights of colour.

romantic ruffled blouse

The romantic frills of organza that cascade down the front of this pin-tucked blouse give it a dramatic look that could be dressed up with a silk skirt for the evening or paired with jeans for daytime.

YOU WILL NEED
silk blouse with pin-tucked front
sewing kit
25cm × 1.5m (10in × 1⅔yd) silk
   chiffon
matching sewing thread
sewing machine

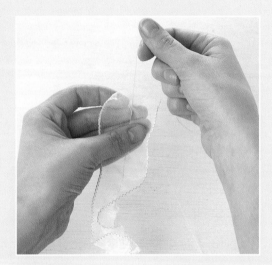

1 Cut six 5 x 70cm (2 x 27in) strips of the chiffon. Machine stitch, using a wide zigzag setting, along both sides of each strip. Sew a line of long straight stitches down the centre of each strip, then pull up one of the threads to create the gathers. Neaten the raw ends by tucking them under and slip stitching down by hand (see page 102).

2 Pin one end of the first ruffle to the shoulderline of the blouse, at the top of a pin tuck. Adjust the gathers so that it is the same length as the tuck and pin, then tack in place. Machine stitch, using a narrow zigzag setting, along the centre. Add two more ruffles to the front panel in the same way, then sew the remaining three to the other panel. Remove the tacking threads.

patchwork hem skirt

*Remnants of fine cotton lawn left over from a quilting project have been torn
into narrow strips and sewn randomly around the edge of a full cotton summer skirt
to give it individual style.*

YOU WILL NEED

white skirt

sewing kit

remnants of lightweight cotton
    fabric

matching sewing thread

sewing machine

1 Press the cotton fabric, then tear it
along the grain into strips of about
15mm (¾in) wide. Cut the strips into
lengths of between 10 and 15cm (4
and 6 in), then fray the cut ends to
match the torn sides.

2 Pin the first strip vertically to the hem
and machine stitch close to the edge.
Add the other strips at random angles,
overlapping some of them, around the
lower part of the skirt.

summer vest top

Evoking summertime pleasures such as trips to the seaside, the scoop neckline of this vest top is encrusted with ricrac starfish, rosettes made from a bright Provençale print and an eclectic selection of buttons.

1 Catch together a loop of ricrac braid to form the first 'arm' of the starfish, over stitching at the centre (see page 103). One by one, form four more loops and stitch in place at the centre to create a five-armed starfish. Trim and neaten the ends. Sew the starfish to the neck of the vest top, tucking the raw ends to the back.

YOU WILL NEED

scoop-neck vest top
sewing kit
30cm (12in) ricrac braid
remnant of toning patterned
  fabric
iron
buttons in matching colours

2 To make a rosette, cut a 4 x 12cm (1¼in x 5in) strip of fabric. Turn under 6mm (¼in) at one short end and press, then press the strip in half lengthways. Align the folded short end with the raw short end and stitch together. Run a gathering thread along the raw edges of the long side. Pull up the thread tightly and secure the rosette with a few stitches.

3 Make more rosettes and starfish and sew them at intervals around the neckline and to the shoulder straps. Stitch the buttons to the rosette centres and in the spaces between the rosettes and starfish (see page 103).

appliquéd hearts t-shirt

Even the smallest scraps from your rag bag can be used to jazz up a plain t-shirt. The two rows of heart motifs have an enduring appeal but plain squares or simple flower shapes would look just as effective.

YOU WILL NEED

cotton t-shirt

sewing kit

pencil, tracing paper and
    scrap paper

scraps of six different cotton
    fabrics

fabric marker pen

tear-off backing paper

sewing machine

matching sewing threads

1 Trace the heart template from page 106 on to paper and cut it out. Using this as a guide, cut six hearts from the different fabrics. The quickest method is to draw around the edge with the marker pen directly on to the fabric and cut around the outline.

2 Find the centre front of the t-shirt by folding it in half vertically, then arrange the hearts in two rows of three. Align the centre of the middle hearts with the centre of the t-shirt. Pin each one down, making sure they are evenly spaced.

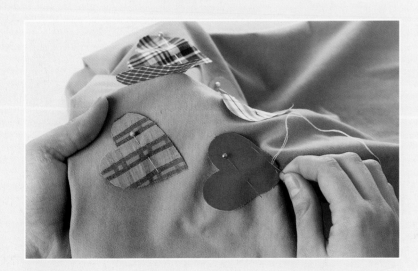

3 Tack the hearts in place, then tack a rectangle of tear-off backing paper, large enough to cover all the tacking stitches, to the wrong side of the t-shirt. Machine stitch around the edge of each heart. Use satin stitch and change threads to match the various fabrics. Remove the backing paper and tacking threads.

decorative cropped trousers

Neutral shades of stone, textured woven fabrics and natural mother-of-pearl blend harmoniously to make a sophisticated trim for a pair of loose cotton trousers.

YOU WILL NEED

cropped cotton trousers

sewing kit

iron

remnants of three different
  fabrics in toning colours, each
  approximately
  5 × 80cm (2 × 32in)

matching sewing thread

sewing machine

approximately 40 shirt buttons

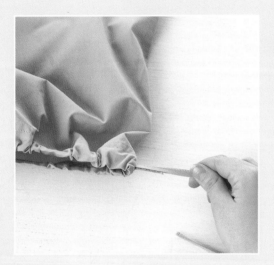

1 Prepare the trousers by taking out any elastic or drawstrings from the hems. Press them well to remove any creases.

2 Measure around the hem then, for the first leg, cut three strips of fabric, each about 2cm (¾in) longer than the hem measurement. Pin and tack the long edges of the fabric strips together, then machine stitch leaving a 6mm (¼in) seam allowance. Unpick the tacking threads.

3 Press the seam allowances outwards on the wrong side, then top stitch 3mm (⅛in) from each edge of the centre strip. Tack and press under a 6mm (¼in) turning along both long edges and one short edge. Stitch 3mm (⅛in) in along the fold of the short edge.

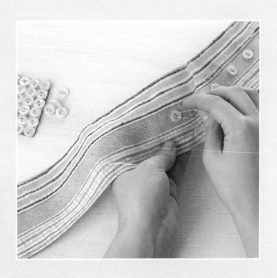

4 Starting 3cm (1¼in) from the neatened end, mark a series of points at 3cm (1¼in) intervals along the centre strip. Sew a button securely to each point (see page 103).

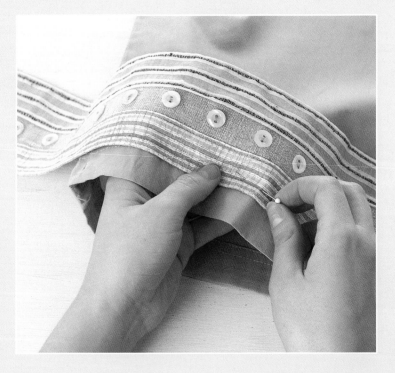

5 Position the completed band just above the hem of the trousers, and pin and tack it in place, following the existing stitching to keep it level. Place the raw end 12mm (½in) from the inside leg seam and overlap it with the neatened end. Machine stitch in place, then sew a final button over the join. Remove the tacking threads. Finish the other leg in the same way.

corsage jacket

A remnant of hand-woven wool and a sample swatch from a traditional weaving mill suggested the embellishment on this peacock blue jacket. Fringed and raw edges add to the unstructured look and complement the simple lines of the garment.

1 Snipping along the grain of the fabric, cut a 2cm (¾in) wide strip of plaid tweed to fit around the collar, plus an extra 5cm (2in) for seam allowances. Pull away the long threads carefully at one side to create an 8mm (⅓in) fringe.

YOU WILL NEED
plain woollen jacket
sewing kit
remnant of plaid tweed
tracing paper, pencil and scrap
    paper
four scraps of different-coloured
    tweed, approximately 15cm
    (6in) square
flower stamens
brooch pin
self-cover buttons to match
    size and number of buttons
    on jacket

2 Starting at the neck edge, pin the strip to the wrong side of the collar so that 3mm (⅛in) of fabric and the fringed edge are visible. Over stitch, sewing between the cut threads to prevent them becoming unravelled (see page 103). Remove the pins as you stitch.

3 Trace the corsage template from page 106 and cut out a paper pattern. Use this as a guide to cut out four plain flowers and one plaid one.

4 Pin three plain flowers together. Place the remaining plain one below the plaid flower and run a gathering stitch around the centre through both fabric layers, following the circle on the template. Pull up the thread and sew a few stamens to the centre. Stitch the gathered flower on top of the other flowers through all layers and sew a brooch pin to the back.

5 Cut off the buttons from the front of the jacket. Following the manufacturer's instructions, make up the self-cover buttons using the left-over plaid tweed. Sew them securely in place (see page 103). Pin the corsage to one shoulder.

accessories

calico shopper

This fabric shopper, which can be easily folded away, is a decorative and eco-conscious alternative to using endless plastic carrier bags. It is decorated with broderie perse, a type of appliqué first used in the eighteenth century to preserve hand-blocked cottons imported from India. The floral motifs were cut out from an old shirt and rearranged to form a new design on a ticking background. They were fixed in place with fusible bonding web and edged by machine, with a narrow zigzag stitch.

fringed flower

The frayed edges of torn strips of organza and cotton lawn give an ethereal quality to this flower corsage. It is made from four strips of fabric: 10 x 50cm (4 x 20in) dark organza; 10 x 40cm (4 x 15in) light organza; 8 x 30cm (3 x 30in) cotton lawn and 6 x 10cm (2½ x 4in) yellow organza. Press each strip in half lengthways and run a gathering thread along the fold. Pull up tightly to make a circle and secure. Place the first three circles together, the largest at the bottom and the smallest at the top, stitch together, then add the flower centre. Sew three velvet leaves and a brooch pin to the wrong side.

hexagon belt

Patchwork hexagons are an old favourite, but can be time-consuming and fiddly to stitch. These origami-like versions are much quicker and can be slip stitched together or used individually as on this striped webbing belt. Trace the template on page 106 and use it as a guide to cut out a hexagon from plain fabric. Press it in half from point to point to mark the centre, then press each of the six edges in turn back to this line. Hold the folded shape in place with a few stitches at the centre then sew on a button to cover the stitching. Make as many folded hexagons as you will need to cover the belt, and secure them in place at the corners.

Argyll scarf

A plain cashmere scarf has been given an Argyll border of coloured diamonds cut from an old pink jumper and two rather moth-eaten scarves. Trace the template on page 107 fourteen times on to fusible bonding web, and follow the manufacturer's instructions to cut out the diamonds from coloured woollen fabrics. Arrange them in three rows, as shown, and iron in place. Use a pressing cloth to protect the wool. Edge each shape with machine zigzag stitch worked in a matching sewing thread.

flowers and leaves

Floral motifs, from tiny sprigged prints to bold super-size blooms, are a perennial favourite with fashion and textile designers. The projects in this chapter show how to create floral designs using different materials and techniques. Ribbon flowers embellished with embroidery in glittery metallic threads look beautiful on a denim background, while other projects range from delicate organza blossoms to a photo-print daffodil, and from pretty lace daisies to flamboyant ribbon roses.

dazzling denim jeans

Ribbon flowers, embellished with metallic thread, silver beads and iridescent sequins, transform this old pair of jeans. If you enjoy embroidery, you could continue to add more decoration to the back pockets, waistband and hems.

YOU WILL NEED

denim jeans

sewing kit

6mm (¼in) organza embroidery
    ribbon in three shades

stranded metallic embroidery
    thread

6mm (¼in) star and cup sequins

2mm (¹⁄₁₂in) rocaille beads

1 Mark a series of points around the curve at the top of the pockets on both front legs, 4cm (1½in) from the seam and 4cm (1½in) apart. Using the embroidery ribbon, sew six or seven petals in ribbon stitch (see page 105) radiating from each point. Work two dark, two medium and two light flowers in ribbon stitch.

2 Using one strand of the metallic embroidery thread, sew a single straight stitch in each of the spaces between the petals.

3 Sew a cup sequin, anchored by a bead, to the centre of each flower and stitch on a bead at the end of the straight stitches (see page 105). Stitch star-shaped sequins between the flowers, securing each one with five small stitches between the points.

garland jacket

For a spring wedding or other special occasion, add a touch of vintage glamour to a plain jacket. Wear it over a simple shift dress in a matching colour for a smartly co-ordinated outfit imbued with 1950's style.

YOU WILL NEED

plain coloured collarless jacket

sewing kit

sheer fabric in green and two
   flower colours

matching sewing threads

1 Cut a 5 x 30cm (2 x 12in) strip of one of the flower colour fabrics. Press in half lengthways and trim a 4cm (1¼in) curve along each open corner. Join the cut edges with a gathering thread and pull it up. Roll the gathers into a flower shape and secure at the base with a few stab stitches. Trim the excess fabric.

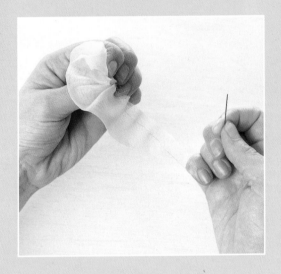

3 Make 12 flowers in each colour and arrange them symmetrically on either side of the jacket front and around the back of the neckline. Pin them in place, then stitch down each one in turn. Remove the pins.

2 For each leaf, cut a rectangle of green fabric about 5 x 10cm (2 x 4in). Press in half lengthways, then fold down the corners to make a triangle and press again. Run a gathering stitch through all layers along the raw edge and pull up the thread to form the leaf. Sew one or two leaves to the back of each flower.

FLOWERS AND LEAVES

daisy cardigan

This sweet guipure lace trim looks like a daisy chain and the flowers can be snipped apart individually without them fraying. Sewn along the ribbed hem of a sky-blue cardigan, the trim adds an appealing freshness and lifts the cardigan out of the ordinary.

1 Snip off the first flower from the lace and cut away any loose threads that are still attached to the motif.

YOU WILL NEED
fine knit cardigan
sewing kit1m (1yd) guipure lace
   trim
matching sewing thread

2 Place the flower at the top of the rib, next to the front edge. Secure the centre with a round of back stitches (see page 102), then sew another circle of stitches half-way along the petals. Continue, attaching more daisies all the way around the cardigan.

daffodil print blouse

This quick and easy project, which uses iron-on transfer paper to print an image on to fabric, involves no sewing at all, and can be completed in an afternoon. A spring daffodil is used here but you could use a photograph of any other flower or motif.

YOU WILL NEED
loose cotton blouse
photograph of a flower head
3 sheets of iron-on transfer
   paper
scissors
iron

1 Digitise, or photocopy, the flower image to make eight repeats. Print them on to the transfer paper so that there are eight images on each of the three sheets. Cut out the images close to the edge of the petals.

2 Following the manufacturer's instructions for the iron-on transfer paper, place a cut-out flower face down on the blouse and iron the back. Peel off the backing paper to reveal the image. Repeat 12 times on each front panel of the blouse.

flamenco evening skirt

Indulge your inner flamenco dancer with this exuberant flower-decked skirt! Wire-edged ribbon makes wonderful, three-dimensional blooms and the subtle ombré colourway lends additional depth to the petals.

YOU WILL NEED
long skirt
sewing kit
4m (4½yds) of 4cm (1½in) wide
   wire-edged, ombré ribbon
iron
matching sewing thread
4m (80in) of 2cm (¾in) wide
   green grosgrain ribbon
3mm (⅛in) rocaille beads to
   match skirt

1 Cut the ombré ribbon into five lengths of approximately 40cm (16in). Pull out the wire carefully from the dark edge of two or three of the ribbons and the light edge of the remaining ribbons.

2 To make a flower, fold the raw ends of the ribbon, so that they lie along the edge without wire to form a triangular point, and press flat. Thread a needle with a length of matching thread. Run a line of gathering stitches along the un-wired edge of the ribbon, draw it up tightly and fasten off.

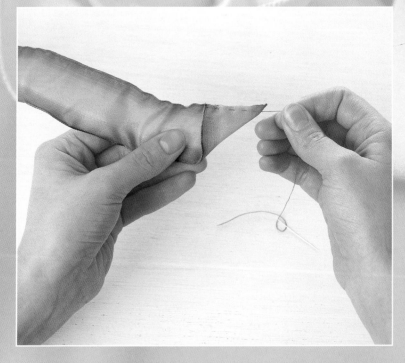

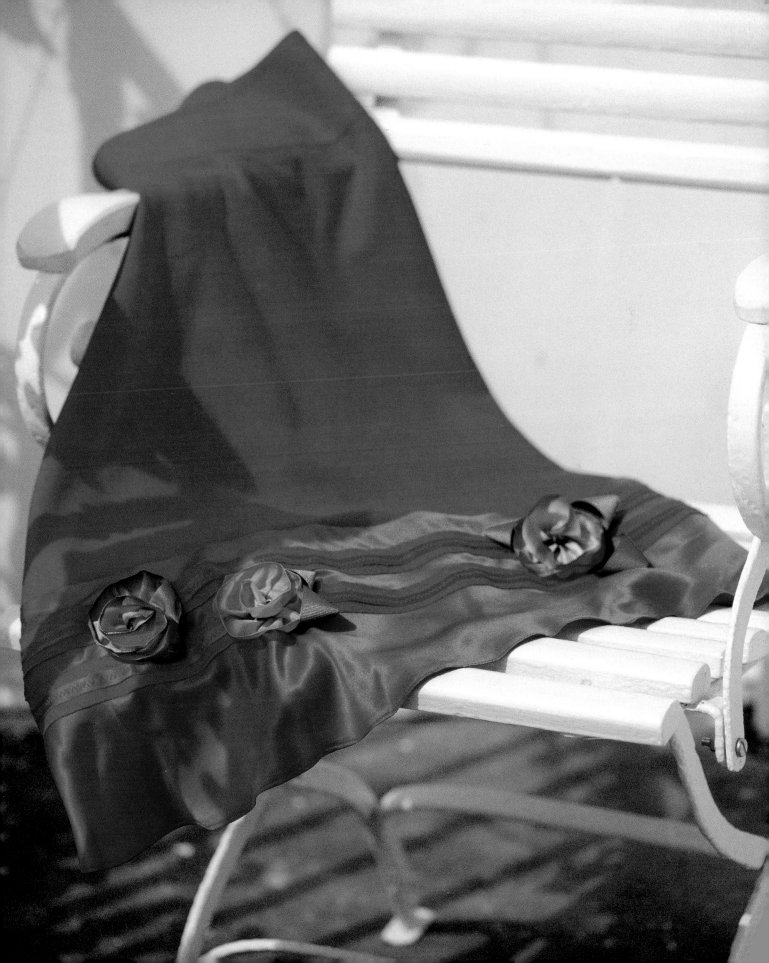

4 Cut a 10cm (4in) length of green ribbon and sew the two ends together to form a pointed loop. Stitch the ends to the back of a flower, then add one or two more leaves. Do the same with the other flowers.

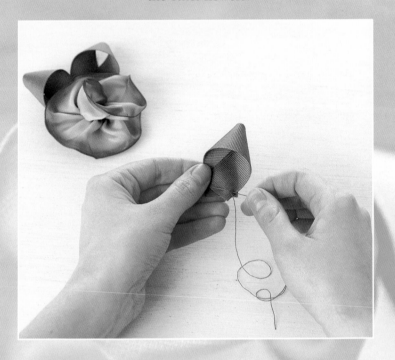

3 Coil the gathered ribbon once around one of the folded ends and secure it with a few stitches. Wrap it around once again and stitch in place, then fold and sew the remaining gathers around the centre to complete the flower. Make up the other ribbon flowers in the same way.

5 Sew the flowers at different heights along the hem of the skirt, alternating the colours. Add a few rocaille beads to conceal any visible stitches and to add highlights of colour (see page 105).

flower power top

This imaginative top looks complicated at first glance, but is made simply by stitching together two similar vest tops. Choose contrasting colours for a bold statement, or toning shades if you prefer a more subtle style.

1 Trace the flower template on page 108, enlarging it as necessary, depending on the size of the garment. Slip one vest inside the other, making sure the straps and hems are aligned. Pin the paper flower to the centre front of the vest tops, and draw around the edge of the flower with a fabric marker pen.

YOU WILL NEED
2 vest tops
sewing kit
tracing paper and pencil
fabric marker pen
tear-off backing paper
sewing machine
matching sewing thread
scrap of contrast cotton jersey
short bugle beads

2 Tack the front parts of the two tops together around the flower template, 6mm (¼in) from the edge of the paper.

3 Unpin the template and turn the vests wrong side out. Tack a square of tear-off backing paper over the motif, turn the vests right side out and machine stitch along the outline of the flower. Use sharp-bladed scissors to snip away the top layer of the flower, cutting close to the stitches.

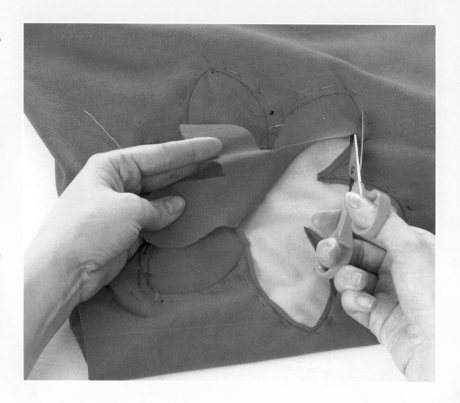

5 Remove the backing paper gently from the wrong side of the fabric, taking care not to pull the stitches. Unpick the tacking thread.

4 Cut a small circle from the contrast jersey and stitch it to the centre of the flower. Sew on a scattering of beads, securing each one with a double stitch (see page 105).

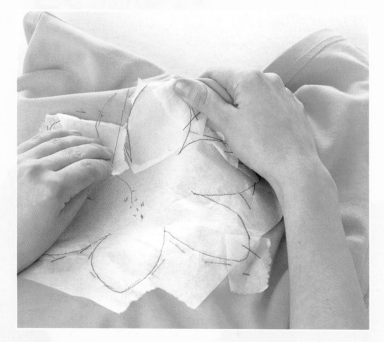

accessories

beaded flower brooch

To make this shimmering flower, a purple gerbera made up of alternate layers of gauzy and silky petals was carefully taken apart. One set of petals was used as a guide to cut out a matching flower shape from toning craft felt. Tiny silver beads were then stitched around the edge of one of the organza flower shapes and the whole flower reassembled with the felt underneath. An antique button was stitched to the centre and a brooch pin to the back.

rosy straw bag

The best silk flowers are often expensive so, for a cheap and cheerful solution, look for substitutes in popular clothing chains and pound stores. These roses were originally attached to hair decorations and – like the straw bag that came from the same shop – were a bargain. The elastic ties were removed and the flowers fixed in place around the top edge of the bag using a cold glue gun.

floral summer sandals

A similar method was used to decorate this pair of gold beach shoes. The blue flowers formed part of a silk hydrangea head, which was dismantled into individual florets, and the pink flowers came from a sprig of fabric blossom. Starting with the largest flower in the middle, each one was glued along the straps. For a pretty finishing touch glittering beads were added to the centres of the largest flowers.

violet hair comb

My grandmother often wore a corsage of faux violets like these on the lapel of her tweed overcoat. I was delighted to find a new bunch with which to make a hair ornament that would be perfect for a bridesmaid. Separate the individual flowers and wind the wire stalks between the teeth of a plastic comb. Leave a longer stem on some of the flowers, so that they will stand up further. Conceal the wires and make sure that no sharp ends protrude by binding green velvet ribbon around the top of the comb. Hand stitch the leaves to the back of the comb.

yarn and wool

The projects on the following pages prove that yarns are no longer just for knitting or crochet. Many new, textured yarns are now available that can be used in exciting ways, and the chapter includes clever ideas for giving traditional garments such as a tailored jacket or tweed skirt a fresh, contemporary look. Some of the most popular embroidery stitches are used to create varied designs and you can even discover how to make your own woollen braid from tapestry yarn, a luxurious collar with a faux-fur effect, and how to 'draw' intricate motifs with couching.

fur-collared jacket

Textile technology has recently produced fantastic new ranges of textured yarns. This brown wool knits up to resemble fake fur, but you could opt for a more vivid, off-beat colour to match a brighter jacket.

YOU WILL NEED
wool jacket with collar
sewing kit
2 × 50g balls of novelty yarn
knitting needles to match weight
    of yarn
matching sewing thread

1 Assess the shape and size of the collar on your chosen jacket. Check the tension guide on the yarn band to find out how many stitches and rows make a 10cm (4in) square. Cast on enough stitches to fit the bottom of the collar, then increase and decrease the number accordingly as you knit. Record the pattern worked as far as the centre back, then reverse the order for the second half.

2 Pin the completed collar on the jacket, then stitch it in place around the outer edge and along the fold. Remove the pins as you sew.

TIP This is a project for an experienced knitter. A simpler option would be to knit a long strip and tuck it under the collar to fit.

tweed skirt with lace detail

Give a demure wool skirt a more enticing look with lace trim around the hem and extra lace and button detailing on the wide waistband.

YOU WILL NEED

tweed skirt

sewing kit

dark lace to fit around hem plus
   an extra 15cm (6in)

light-coloured felt

1 large and 2 small black
   buttons

sewing machine (optional)

1 Cut a motif from the lace, then cut out a slightly smaller piece of felt. Holding this behind the lace, tack both layers to one side of the waistband. Hand stitch around the edge of the lace and work a few stab stitches across the centre. Add a second motif to the other side of the waistband in the same way. Unpick the tacking.

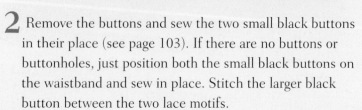

2 Remove the buttons and sew the two small black buttons in their place (see page 103). If there are no buttons or buttonholes, just position both the small black buttons on the waistband and sew in place. Stitch the larger black button between the two lace motifs.

3 Pin the remaining lace around the hem. To accommodate the curve of the hem, you may need to snip into the lace at intervals. Sew by hand, or with a sewing machine set to a narrow zigzag.

lacy embroidered cardigan

Make a feminine cardigan even prettier by adding tiny embroidered flowers in shades of pink and faux pearls, carefully chosen to match the background colour. Two vintage buttons at the front are a perfect finishing touch.

1 Using all six strands of the thread and a tapestry needle, work a lazy daisy stitch flower (see page 104) at the point of the knitted design. Depending on the pattern, make another flower at every other point in the row, then at alternate points on the next row across the two front panels. Change between the four shades of thread to give a varied effect.

YOU WILL NEED
lace knit cardigan
sewing kit
four skeins of stranded
    embroidery thread in shades
    of the same colour
tapestry needle
4mm (⅛in) pearl beads
matching sewing thread
replacement buttons

2 Add a pearl bead to the centre of each flower, securing it with sewing thread to match the cardigan (see page 105).

3 Snip off the buttons and replace them with vintage versions or attractive new buttons to complement the embroidery (see page 103).

stripy flower top

Yarn can be used in a graphic way to 'draw' motifs on a garment. Textured chenille yarn is couched with small stitches to create the flowers and tendrils that adorn this stripy vest.

YOU WILL NEED

striped vest top

sewing kit

heat transfer pencil and thin
    paper

iron

matching sewing thread

chenille and textured yarns in
    four colours

4mm (⅙in) pearl beads

1 Enlarge the flower templates on page 107 according to how big you want the design to be on your garment. Use the heat transfer pencil to trace the outlines on to thin paper. Cut out the motifs roughly, then position them on the vest top. Press with a hot iron to transfer the outlines to the fabric, following the manufacturer's instructions.

2 Thread a needle with thread to match the first yarn. Hold the yarn along the transferred outline and couch it down with small stitches (see page 104). Outline all the flowers and tendrils in the same way using different colours.

3 Finish each flower by sewing a few pearl beads to the centre space (see page 105).

braided tweed jacket

Coco Chanel first added woollen braid to tweed to produce her signature look. To give a jacket couture styling, plait your own customised version from tapestry yarn selected to complement the colours of the fabric.

YOU WILL NEED

tweed jacket

sewing kit

6 skeins of tapestry yarn in
three toning colours (two
of each)

masking tape

matching sewing thread

1 Measure the top of the jacket pocket and cut four pieces of each yarn to two and a half times this length. Knot all twelve strands at one end, then tape the knot to your work surface and plait them together.

2 Bind the loose ends of the plait with a few stitches, then trim to 6mm (¼in). Fold the tuft behind the plait and secure with a few unobtrusive stitches. Neaten the other end so that the braid fits exactly along the pocket top.

3 Pin the braid 3cm (1¼in) down from the top of the pocket and secure it along each edge with small, tight stitches. Remove the pins.

4 Snip off the button from the cuff and sew it to the centre of the braid (see page 103).

5 Measure the collar and lapels and make a plait two-and-a-half times this length. Neaten one end of the plait and pin it to the wrong side of the jacket, level with the first buttonhole. Pin the braid around the lapels and collar and stitch in place. Trim and neaten the loose end.

embroidered shrug

The seemingly intricate design of twining flowers and leaves on this cotton top is created using just four easily-worked embroidery stitches. Embroidery threads are available in myriad shades to complement any garment.

1 Thread a tapestry needle with the lighter green cotton and work a wavy line of chain stitch along each front edge of the garment. Instructions for all the embroidery stitches used to decorate the shrug are given on pages 104–105. For a knitted garment, take the needle through the spaces between the knitted stitches.

YOU WILL NEED

striped bolero or short-sleeved
shrug
10 skeins of embroidery cotton
in co-ordinating colours,
including two shades of two
of the same colours for the
flowers and leaves
tapestry needle
scissors

2 The leaves are made by working a detached chain stitch over a single straight stitch. Sew the leaves in pairs, at regular intervals, on either side of the curving stem.

3 Work the flowers in the same way as the leaves. Here, pink cotton was used to stitch two slanting petals that meet at the base. Two different shades of pink give variety to the design.

4 Work two fly stitches at the base of each pair of petals, using the darker green thread.

5 In different colours, sew a cluster of five or more French knots between the petals of each flower. Add a few single French knots in the spaces between the flowers and leaves.

accessories

pansy drawstring bag

This soft felt bag could be used to protect a spectacle case. Glue a band of felt to one edge of a 20cm (8in) square of dark felt. Using the template on page 109, cut the petals from craft felt and sew them to the middle of the band with blanket stitch worked in pearl cotton. Stitch two small circles of felt to the flower centre with a few long stitches. With right sides together join the side edges of the felt square. Fold the bag so that the seam lies at the centre back and stitch across the bottom. Turn through. Use a large needle to thread two lengths of cotton tape through the top edge, to make the drawstrings. Add a couple of beads to each end and knot securely.

bobble hat and scarf

Use the templates on page 109 to cut out two cardboard rings. You will need one large pompom for the hat and 10 small ones for the scarf. Thread a tapestry needle with three long lengths of wool. Holding the rings together in one hand, pass the needle through the centre, around the outside edge, and back through the centre. Continue around the card until the centre space is filled. Push a pair of sharp scissors between the rings and snip through the loops of wool. Ease the rings slightly apart, slip a length of wool between them and wrap it twice round the centre. Knot the ends tightly. Pull off the rings, then trim the pompom into a neat ball.

felt flowers

Anyone who has ever accidentally machine washed their favourite jumper on a too-high setting will know what happens when you boil pure woollen knitwear. The fibres shrink and the fabric becomes thick and dense. If you have any woollens that are no longer fit to be worn, you can wash them at 90 degrees celsius and create your own felt. Using the templates on page 109, cut three flowers and three flower centres from felted wool. Roll up the flower centres and stitch to the petals, gathering the petals slightly. Cut six leaves and three stalks from green craft felt. Roll up the stalks, slip stitch the long edges, then sew the flowers and leaves to the stalks. Tie the three flowers together with a scrap of ribbon. Attach a brooch pin or fix the flowers to a basket with a cold glue gun.

key charm

You will never misplace your keys when they are secured to this fashionable key ring, made from leftover wool and a few glass beads. Make a tassel by winding a length of yarn 30 times around a 5cm (2in) wide strip of card. Slip three 30cm (12in) strands, each a different colour, under the loop, and slide it off the card. Form the tassel head by binding another length of yarn below the point held by the strands and fasten off. Cut the loop at the bottom to form the tassel ends. Plait the long strands for 4cm (1½in), then slide two beads on to each and secure. Make another two tassels in different colours and plait all three tassels together. Attach a spring fastener or a split ring to the top of the plait.

practicalities

sewing techniques

You don't have to be an experienced dressmaker to customise your clothes: the needlework skills required are straightforward and easy to learn. The following instructions and illustrations will guide you through all the sewing and embroidery stitches used in the step-by-step projects, and may even give you some more ideas.

running stitch

This stitch has many uses. Seam two edges together with short running stitches, about 3mm (⅛in) in length. To work a gathering thread, sew a line of longer stitches – 8mm (⅓in) or more – and pull up the thread to create the frill. Even larger stitches, about 12mm (½in) in length, are used for tacking (basting) a seam before machine stitching.

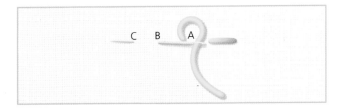

Bring the needle up at A, insert it at B and bring it out again at C. Continue in this way, making evenly spaced stitches of equal length.

> ### measuring up
> The amount of fabric, lace or ribbon needed for any of the projects will depend on the particular garment that is to be embellished. For this reason, no precise quantities are given in many of the instructions, so measure up carefully before buying any trimmings and allow a little extra.

back stitch

Back stitch can be worked in straight or curved lines for both practical seaming and embroidery.

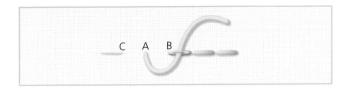

Bring the needle up at A and take it back to the right, inserting the point at B. Come up at C, equidistant from A, and insert the needle again at A to make the second back stitch. Continue to the end of the row, keeping the stitches equal in length.

slip stitch

This almost invisible stitch is used to sew lace or ribbon in place or to appliqué a motif on to a background fabric.

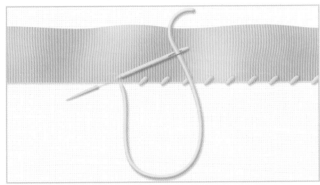

Bring the needle up through the background fabric, just below the ribbon. Take it down through the ribbon, close to the edge and come back through the fabric, no further than 6mm (¼in) along, to make the second stitch. Continue to the end, being careful not to pull the thread too tightly.

over stitch

Use this stitch to sew beaded motifs, as well as cut out shapes without a seam allowance, in place. The thread overlaps the raw edges and prevents any fraying.

Start the first stitch inside the motif, about 3mm (⅛in) from the edge. Take it down through the background fabric at an angle, keeping the needle close to the raw edge. Repeat all the way around the motif.

sewing on a button

Secure the thread at the point where the button is to be attached. Pass the needle up through one of the holes, back down through the other hole and through the fabric. Work four to six more stitches, then fasten off with back stitch behind the button. On buttons with four holes, sew two parallel sets of stitches or work the stitches in a cross.

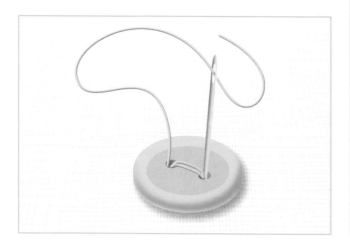

turning up a hem

If you want to neaten a raw edge or shorten a skirt or a pair of trousers you will need to make a hem. Mark the finished length with a line of pins. Press under a narrow turning along the raw edge then fold the fabric so that the crease lies along the pinned line. Pin or tack the fold, then sew in place by machine or by hand with hem stitch.

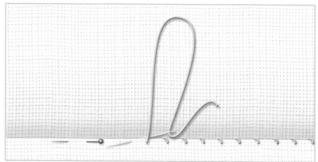

Start by bringing the needle up through the fold. Pick up one or two threads of fabric from the other side, just above the hem, then bring the needle back through the hem. Repeat to the end, taking care not to make the stitches too tight. Remove the pins or tacking.

caring for your clothes

Embellished garments will require special attention when it comes to laundering and pressing. It is worth taking a little extra care to preserve your hard work. If in doubt, go to a specialist dry cleaner. Beaded items can be machine washed on a low setting if the beads were labelled by the manufacturer as washable. To be on the safe side, however, hand wash garments in warm water, then squeeze out excess moisture gently and dry flat. Avoid tumble-drying any decorated items and always iron on the wrong side with a cool iron. Take special care when pressing any garment decorated with sequins – they may melt!

embroidery stitches

For decorative embroidery, there is a wealth of stitches from which to choose. On these pages you will find instructions for those used in the projects. The stitches can be combined with beads, sequins and appliqué or used individually to create new designs. Experiment with different threads, colours, scale and texture.

couching

You can 'draw' on to fabric with a cord or thick yarn by anchoring it with small stitches worked in fine thread. Bring a needle threaded with sewing cotton up at A and take it down at B over the thick thread. Come back up at C and continue making evenly spaced stitches at right angles. Maintain tension by holding the couched thread down with the tip of your thumb as you stitch.

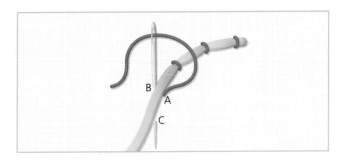

fly stitch

Also known as 'Y' stitch because of its shape, this is a good partner for lazy daisy stitch. Make a loose stitch from A to B. Bring the needle out over the thread at C and take it back down at D to complete a single upright stitch. For a border, start the next stitch at E.

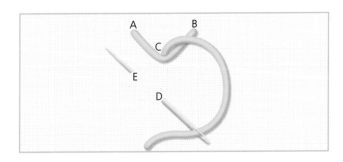

chain stitch

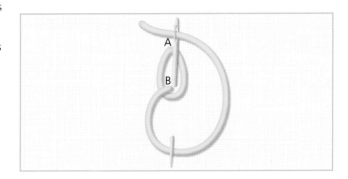

This versatile stitch is made up of interlinked loops, and is useful for lettering and spirals as well as curved lines. Bring the needle up at A. Loop the thread from left to right and hold it down with a thumb. Re-insert the needle at A and bring the point up at B, over the loop. Pull the thread through gently, then insert the needle at B, ready to make the next stitch.

lazy daisy stitch

Embroider a circle of chain stitch 'petal" to make a flower or just one to form a leaf.

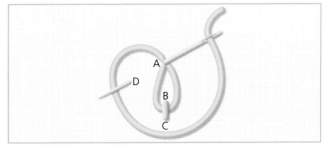

Bring the needle up at A. Loop the thread from left to right and hold it down with a thumb. Re-insert the needle at A and bring the point up at B. Take it over the loop and anchor with a small stitch from B to C. Make the next petal from A to D and continue clockwise to complete the flower.

French knot

This round knot is easier than it looks: the secret is to use a fine needle that will slip easily through the loops and to maintain the tension. Bring the needle up at A. Hold the working thread taut and, with the other hand, twist the point of the needle twice around the thread. Take it back down at B and pull the thread through, leaving a knot on the surface.

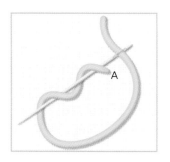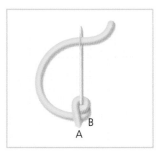

ribbon stitch (*see diagram below left*)

Silk embroidery ribbons make pretty three-dimensional flowers. Thread the ribbon through a crewel needle and bring it up at A. Holding it down lightly at C, take the needle down through the centre at B. Pull the ribbon through slowly so that it turns back on itself to form a petal.

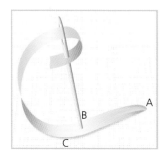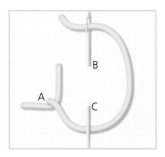

blanket stitch (*see diagram above right*)

Bring the needle up at A, then take it down at B and come up directly below, or under the edge of the fabric, at C, over the working thread. Pull the thread through and repeat to the end, finishing with a small straight stitch.

sewing on beads and sequins

To sew a bead in place – bring the needle up at A and thread on the bead. Take the needle down at B, far enough from A for the bead to lie flat on the fabric. To ensure the bead is secure, pass the thread through the bead once again.

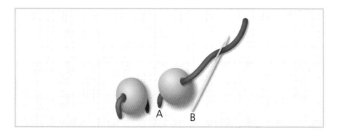

To anchor a sequin with a bead – bring the needle up at A and thread on the sequin followed by a small bead. Take the needle back down through the hole in the sequin. Make a second stitch to ensure the sequin and bead are firmly attached.

To sew on a single sequin – bring the needle up at A and thread on the sequin. Take the needle down at B, so that the sequin lies flat.

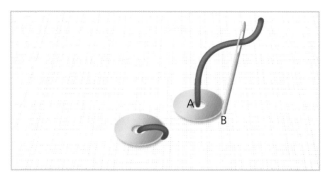

Butterfly shrug
(pages 21–23)

Hexagon belt
(page 64)

Appliquéd hearts t-shirt
(pages 56–57)

Corsage jacket
(pages 61–63)

Stripy flower top
(pages 92–93)

Argyll scarf
(page 64)

Silver-beaded jeans pocket
(pages 24–25)

Flower power top
(pages 79–81)

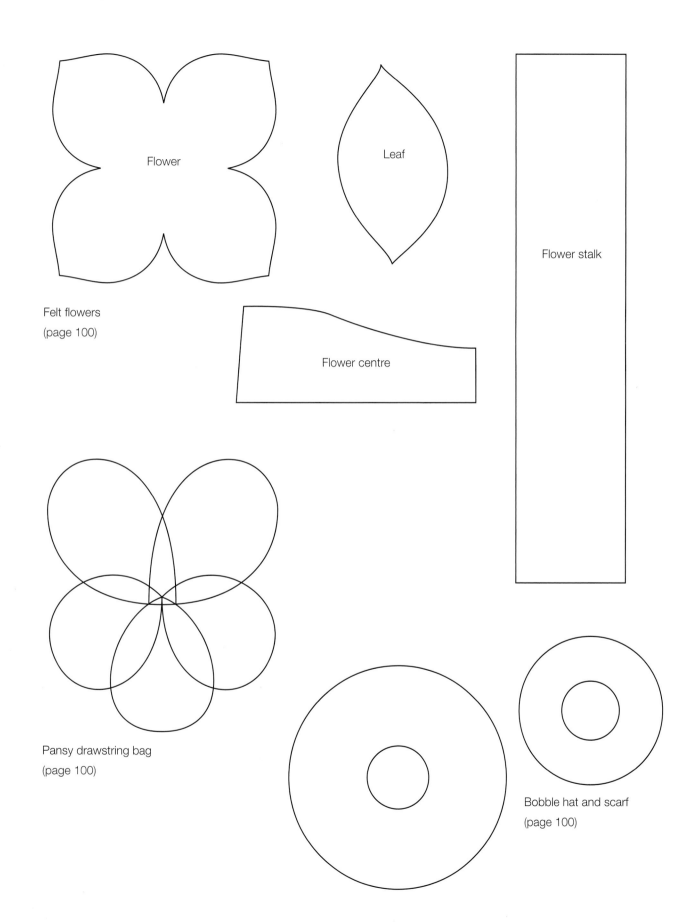

Flower

Leaf

Flower stalk

Felt flowers
(page 100)

Flower centre

Pansy drawstring bag
(page 100)

Bobble hat and scarf
(page 100)

SUPPLIERS

The Bead Shop
21a Tower Street
London WC2H 9NS
Tel: 020 7240 0931
www.beadshop.co.uk

Fantastic selection of beads, sequins and jewellery findings.

Bedecked Limited
Wernwen Farm
Craswall
Hereford HR2 OPP
Tel: 01981 510384
www.bedecked.co.uk

Online range of trimmings, haberdashery and accessories.

Berwick Offray
Tel: 01844 9735196 for stockist details
www.offray.com

Leading manufacturer of ribbons, available nationwide from good fabric, craft and hobby stores.

Cloth House
47 Berwick Street
London
W1F 8SJ
Tel: 020 7437 5155
www.clothhouse.com

Unusual fabrics, from silk and velvet to linen and brocade.

Creative Beadcraft
(Ells and Farrier)
20 Beak Street
London
W1F 9RE
Tel: 01494 715606
www.creativebeadcraft.co.uk

Beads, sequins, diamantés and more.

Delicate Stitches
339 Kentish Town Road
London
NW5 2TJ
Tel: 0870 203 2323
www.londonbeadco.co.uk

A treasure trove of haberdashery, trimmings and beads.

DMC
Tel: 0116 2811040 for stockist details
www.dmc.com

Manufacturers of embroidery threads and tapestry yarn.

Gütermann
Tel: 020 8589 1635 for stockist details
www.gutermann.com

Good range of sequins, rocaille, bugle and larger beads.

Ilona Biggins
PO Box 600
Rickmansworth
WD3 5WR
Tel: 01923 282998
www.ilonabiggins.co.uk

Beautiful beads, pearls and gemstones.

John Lewis
www.johnlewis.com

The definitive haberdashery department, plus a good selection of dressmaking fabrics.

Liberty
Regent Street
London W1
020 7732 1234
www.liberty.co.uk

Haberdashery and fabrics, including classic Liberty tana lawn.

Nichols Buttons
www.nicholsbuttons.co.uk

Unique vintage hand-made buttons.

New Rainbow Textiles
98 The Broadway
Southall
Middlesex
UB1 1QF
Tel: 020 8574 1494

Sari fabrics, braids and silks.

Nostalgia
147a Nottingham Road
Eastwood
Nottingham
NG16 3GJ
Tel: 01773 712240
www.nostalgiaribbon.com

Unusual and beautiful trims and embellishments, including Mokuba ribbons and velvet flowers.

Ribbon Moon
www.ribbonmoon.co.uk

Online haberdashery store, with a choice of over 3,500 different buttons.

VV Rouleaux
54 Sloane Square
Cliveden Place
London
SW1 8AW
Tel: 020 7730 3125
www.vvrouleaux.com

An unrivalled selection of ribbon, cords, braids, feathers, tassels and ready-made trimmings.

Index